Arkansas Wildlife

Animals & Mammals

Billy Grinslott & Kinsey Marie Books

ISBN - 9781968228019

Chipmunks are found in many areas. Chipmunks are small members of the squirrel family. They like to eat nuts and seeds. Chipmunks are most active during the day, especially at dawn and dusk. They have pouches inside of their cheeks so they can carry food. They are very friendly and will take food from your hand. Chipmunks need about 15 hours of sleep per day. The smallest chipmunk species is Tamias minimus, which is found throughout North America.

There are many squirrels in the wild. You may see a red or gray squirrel. The most popular is the gray squirrel. Squirrels are very acrobatic and can climb trees. Their favorite food is acorns. Squirrels hide their food in many small stashes and can find more than 90% of them later. Squirrels are fast and can run up a tree at 12 miles per hour. Newborn squirrels are blind, deaf, and hairless, and rely on their mother until they mature.

Flying Squirrels don't fly like birds. They don't have wings. They have skin that is attached to their legs. When they jump from a tree, they spread their legs out and glide through the air. Most glides are 30 feet from tree to tree. But they can glide up to 150 feet. They are primarily active at night and are social animals, often living in groups and sharing nests. They have large eyes for night vision, long whiskers for navigating in the dark, and a long, flattened tail for steering during glides.

Swamp rabbits are fascinating creatures with several unique adaptations for their wetland habitats. They are the largest cottontail in North America, excellent swimmers, and can even hide in the water by only sticking their nose above the surface. They also have a specialized fur coat. Their thick fur is dense and waterproof, helping them stay dry in their wetland environment. They primarily eat reeds and swampy grasses, a diet that requires them to live near water sources.

There are many types of rabbits in the wild. The most common is the cottontail. Rabbits are cute, friendly, and fun to watch. Many people have rabbits for pets. They have soft fluffy fur. They are called cottontails because they have a white fluffy tail that looks like a cotton ball.

Pee-ewe what is that stinky critter with the big bushy tail. It smells bad. Skunks are normally curious and friendly unless you scare them. If you scare them, they will flip their bushy tale at you and spray you with a smelly potion and it stinks. Skunks spray a smelly, sulfur-based liquid from their anal glands as a defense mechanism. The spray can cause eye irritation and temporary blindness. Skunks are highly adaptable and can thrive in many different environments. Skunks have strong forefeet and long claws for digging. Skunks live in dens.

Armadillos are known for their unique armor-like shells. Armadillos are the only living mammals with a hard shell, made of true bone and consisting of bands of plates connected by flexible skin. When threatened they can roll up into a ball and their shell protects them. Armadillos are primarily nocturnal animals, spending their days in burrows and emerging at night to forage for food. They are excellent diggers, using their strong claws and legs to burrow into the ground and forage for food, which primarily consists of insects and grubs. They also like to eat ant and termites.

Opossums or possums have strong tails and can hang from trees. One trick that a possum has, is when it feels danger is it will play dead. It will lay there and not move. Possums have white to gray face hair. Possums like to eat wood ticks. They are also immune to snakebites. Opossums are susceptible to frostbite because their hands and tails are not protected by fur. Opossums are marsupials, which means they have pouches for their young, like kangaroos and koalas.

Raccoons like to come out at night. Their eyes are made so they can see in the dark. Raccoons are highly intelligent and can solve problems. They can learn to open doors, trash cans, and other containers. They are called masked bandits because they like to raid and eat out of trash cans at night. Raccoons can survive in many environments.

Ringtails look like a racoon. They have stripes on their tails, but their face more resembles a cat. They are a member of the racoon family. Ringtails can be found in some parts of North America. Ringtails are excellent climbers capable of ascending vertical walls, trees, rocky cliffs and even cactus. They are mostly nocturnal. Ringtails are agile climbers and leapers, with hind legs that can rotate 180 degrees. Their long tails help with balance. Ringtails have anal glands that produce a foul-smelling secretion.

Groundhogs or woodchucks are the largest member of the squirrel family. Groundhogs get their name because of their big bodies, and they live underground. Groundhogs are skilled climbers and swimmers. Groundhogs are true hibernators, sleeping for up to six months. Groundhog Day is where Punxsutawney Phil predicts how long winter will last.

Otters have the thickest fur of any animal. The otter is one of the few mammals that use tools, like rocks to break thing open. A group of otters resting together is called a raft.

Otters primarily rely on their sense of touch, whiskers, and forepaws, in murky waters to locate food. Otters have built in pouches of loose skin under their forearms to stash extra food when diving.

Beavers use their teeth to cut and knock down trees. They build dams with them to block water, so they have a place to live and swim. They also eat wood. Beavers can stay underwater for about 8 minutes. Beavers slap their tails on the water to indicate danger. Beavers are the largest rodents in North America.

Plains pocket gophers are burrowing rodents and are known for their digging activities and unique adaptations for underground life. They have very sharp claws for digging. They create complex underground tunnel systems. Their fur-lined cheek pouches, or pockets, are used to store and transport food, like roots, tubers, and grasses, back to their burrows. They can turn their cheek pouches inside out for grooming purposes. Their tails are highly sensitive and act as feelers to help them navigate the dark tunnels, even when backing up.

Badgers have elongated heads, small ears, and black and white faces. Badgers live underground with other family members. Badgers are very social and live in groups. A badger den or sett can be centuries old and are used by many generations of badgers. Badgers are very territorial, it's best not to bother them is you see one. A group of badgers is called a cete, though they are often called clans. Badgers are largely nocturnal but reduce their activity during periods of cold weather.

The American Mink lives across most of North America and is a cat sized. Mink are very skilled climbers and swimmers. They prefer to keep to themselves. They communicate using odors, visual signals, and other sounds. They purr when they're happy. Mink are agile swimmers, and they often dive to find food

Weasels are the smallest members of the meat-eating animals. Although small, they do not hibernate and are active all winter. Weasels in northern ranges turn white in the winter to camouflage in the snow. Weasels have long whiskers like cats, to help them feel things. They even have long whiskers on their elbows. When a weasel gets annoyed, it stomps its feet, just like humans do. Weasels are quick, agile, and alert animals. They are excellent climbers and swimmers.

Many Lemmings fur can change color with the seasons. Lemmings live in holes and tunnels that they dig in the ground. In winter they tunnel under the snow. Lemmings eat mosses, roots, and grasses. Lemmings are very small animals, usually, just three to six inches long. Their bodies are covered in thick fur and they don't hibernate during winter months.

Fishers live in the forests of Canada and many parts of the United States. They hiss and growl when upset. They are closely related to badgers, mink, and otters. Fisher young are known as kits. Fishers are one of the few animals that eat porcupines. Fishers are also called pekan, pequam, wejack, and woolang.

Mallard ducks are by far the most recognizable and popular ducks in the world. They live in just about every area of North America. Their estimated population is around 19 million birds. The male is easily recognizable from its white neck ring and green neck and head. The female Mallard has between five to 14 light green eggs. Most ducks don't have green eggs, so this makes them unique. The male Mallard is called a drake and the female a hen. Female Mallards quack. Males don't quack, instead they produce deeper, raspier one- and two-note calls. They can also make rattling sounds by rubbing their bills against their flight feathers.

Canada Geese are the most sought after and abundant goose in North America. They live in many places. Canada geese can travel 1,500 miles in a day if the weather permits. Canada geese migrate every year. They fly in a V-formation, which allows them to travel long distances without stopping, as they can switch positions and conserve energy. Canada geese are known for their distinctive honk and are sometimes called Canadian honkers.

Mourning Doves are unable to sweat, to stay cool during hot weather, they pant just like dog do. Mourning doves eat and collect seeds in their crop, which is an enlarged part of their esophagus. Then they digest them later. It's estimated that there are more than 100 million mourning doves in the US. With the southern states having the biggest population.

The bobwhite quail has the largest range of any game bird in America. Bobwhite quail are the most common species of quail, the bobwhite is often referred to as the number one game bird of the eastern and southern United States. Bobwhite quail are known for their explosive flight, and social behavior in groups called coveys.

Ringed Neck Pheasants are one of the most sought-after birds in North America. They are found throughout most of Northern America and Canada. Ring-necked pheasants are not native to the US. Instead, they were brought here from Asia in the 1880's. While not as widespread as quail, they are present in some areas of Arkansas.

The Wild Turkey is a large, bird that is native to North America. It is the heaviest bird in the United States and can weigh up to 24 pounds. Only male turkey's gobble. Wild turkeys can fly. Wild turkeys sleep in trees. Their heads can change colors. You can tell a turkey's emotions by the color of their heads. Colors can change from red to blue to white, depending on how excited or calm they are. You can find wild turkeys in just about every state in America.

The national bird of the United States is the Bald Eagle. Bald eagles are large birds, with females up to 43 inches long and weighing up to 13 pounds. Their wingspan can be up to 7 feet wide. Bald eagles build the largest nests of any bird, up to 13 feet wide and weighing more than half a ton. Bald eagles aren't actually bald. The name bald eagle comes from the old English word piebald bird, which meant white-headed bird. Bald eagles have the best eyesight of any bird. A bald eagle can see up to three miles away, which is about four to five times farther than a human. They can also see small details like an ant on the ground from great distances.

Bobcats are named for their short, bobbed tails with white tips. They have similar markings to lynxes but are much smaller. Bobcats live in a variety of habitats. Bobcats are skilled at leaping and can run up to 30 miles per hour.

The cougar has a number of different names, it's also known as the mountain lion or Puma. They are the fourth largest cat in the world. The cougar has the largest range of any wild cat in the North America. A cougar can jump upward 18 feet from a sitting position. They can leap up to 30 feet horizontally. Cougars cannot roar like a lion, but they can make calls like a human scream.

Gray fox prefers to live in rocky canyons and ridges but can also be found in wooded areas and open fields. They have strong, hooked claws that enable them to climb trees. Which is abnormal for a dog species. Gray foxes are not observed as frequently as red foxes due to their reclusive nature and more nocturnal habits.

Red foxes have excellent hearing, allowing them to hear rodents digging underground from miles away. When afraid, red foxes grin or look like they are smiling. Red foxes front paws have five toes, while their hind feet only have four. Foxes dig underground dens where they raise their kits and hide from predators. A group of foxes is called a skulk or a leash. Babys are called kits and females are called vixens.

The coyote is bigger than a fox weighing between 20 and 45 pounds. Eastern coyotes are part wolf. Coyotes are great for pest control. They like to eat mice and rats. They can adapt and live almost anywhere, even in the city. Coyotes are very smart and have been observed learning and following traffic signals in some cities. They have a yip type of call when they communicate with each other. Coyotes are found in all the United States, except Hawaii.

There have been reports of larger canines being seen in Arkansas, leading to discussions about whether these could be coywolves, which are a result of cross breeding between coyotes and wolves. While coyotes are common, they are smaller than Coywolves. These can be significantly larger than a typical coyote.

The whitetail deer is the most popular deer in North America. Whitetail deer have good eyesight and hearing. They can detect small sounds from a quarter of a mile away. Only male deer grow antlers, which are shed each year. Whitetail deer are good swimmers and will use large streams and lakes to escape predators. A young deer is called a fawn, a male is a buck, and a female is called a doe. They are the most common deer species and live everywhere in North America.

Black bears are the smallest members of the bear family in North America. Black Bears love to eat sweet things like berries, fruits, and vegetables. They are good climbers and fast runners. They are excellent swimmers and can paddle at least a mile and a half in freshwater. They usually sleep for long periods of time and hibernate during the winter. They typically try to stay away from people unless they find food in the area.

Yes, there are feral hogs, often called wild boars, in Arkansas. They are an invasive species found in numerous counties, primarily in the southern third of the state. Feral hogs are also known as wild boars. Feral hogs are known for their high reproductive rates and their tendency to root up the ground, which can lead to habitat destruction. They are highly intelligent, social animals with a keen sense of smell and a surprisingly good memory. Wild pigs can be found in various habitats, including forests, grasslands, and agricultural areas.

Yes, there are elk in Arkansas, primarily found in the Ozark Mountains, particularly along the Buffalo National River. Elk are the second largest members of the deer family. Bulls can weigh up to 1,100 lbs. They can run 40 miles per hour and outrun horses. Elk have eyes on the sides of their heads and can see in every direction except directly in front or behind. They make a cool bugling sound when communicating with other elk. It's fun to listen to them.

Yes, there are bison in Arkansas. Several ranches, like Ozark Valley Bison Farm, in the Ozark Mountains raise bison, Bison are the largest mammal in North America and weigh up to 2,000 pounds. Bison can run up to 35 miles per hour. They can jump 6 feet vertically and more than 7 feet horizontally. Bison calves are nicknamed red dogs, because of their orange-red fur color at birth.

Fun Facts about Arkansas Animals

1 - The state's official mammal is the white-tailed deer, and its population is significant, with an estimated one million deer.

2 - The Northern Mockingbird, one of the most popular birds in the South, became the state bird of Arkansas in 1929.

3 - The black bear is the only species of bear in Arkansas. The black bear population in Arkansas is estimated to be over 5,000 animals.

4 - The largest wild cat in Arkansas is the mountain lion, also known as a cougar or puma. These cats can weigh up to 200 pounds.

5 - Coyotes are the most abundant large predator, and they usually prey on small mammals, rats and mice.

6 - There are roughly 70 wild mammal species known in Arkansas. From small rodents to larger predators and herbivores.

7 - The gray fox is the smallest wild canine, member of the dog family.

8 - Some of the most popular and commonly sighted wild animals include white-tailed deer, wild hogs, black bears, wild turkeys, and bobcats.

Author Page

Billy Grinslott & Kinsey Marie Books

Copyright, All Rights Reserved

ISBN - 9781968228019

Thanks

www.ingramcontent.com/pod-product-compliance
Lightning Source LLC
Chambersburg PA
CBHW060849270326
41934CB00002B/66